W9-CCS-877

WELCOME TO THE WORLD OF ANIMALS

Wolves

Diane Swanson

Gareth Stevens Publishing
MILWAUKEE

For a free color catalog describing Gareth Stevens' list of high-quality books and multimedia programs, call 1-800-542-2595 (USA) or 1-800-461-9120 (Canada). Gareth Stevens Publishing's Fax: (414) 225-0377.
See our catalog, too, on the World Wide Web: http://gsinc.com

The publishers acknowledge the support of the Canada Council for the Arts and the Cultural Services Branch of the Government of British Columbia in making this publication possible.

Library of Congress Cataloging-in-Publication Data

Swanson, Diane, 1944-
    [Welcome to the world of wolves]
    Wolves / by Diane Swanson.
       p. cm. — (Welcome to the world of animals)
    Originally published: Welcome to the world of wolves. North Vancouver, B.C.:
Whitecap Books, © 1996.
    Includes index.
    Summary: Describes the physical characteristics and behavior of wolves.
    ISBN 0-8368-2218-8 (lib. bdg.)
    1. Wolves—Juvenile literature. [1. Wolves.] I. Title. II. Series: Swanson, Diane,
1944- Welcome to the world of animals.
    QL737.C22S835   1998
    599.773—dc21   98-6600

This North American edition first published in 1998 by
Gareth Stevens Publishing
1555 North RiverCenter Drive, Suite 201
Milwaukee, WI 53212 USA

This U.S. edition © 1998 by Gareth Stevens, Inc. Original edition © 1996 by Diane Swanson. First published in 1996 by Whitecap Books, Vancouver/Toronto. Additional end matter © 1998 by Gareth Stevens.

Gareth Stevens series editor: Dorothy L. Gibbs
Editorial assistant: Diane Laska
Cover design: Renee M. Bach

Cover photograph: Victoria Hurst/First Light
Photo credits: Robert Lankinen/First Light 4; Lynn M. Stone 6, 16, 26; Thomas Kitchin/First Light 8, 20, 22, 28; Peter McLeod/First Light 10, 14, 18, 24, 30; Jeff Vanuga/First Light 12.

Printed in Mexico

1 2 3 4 5 6 7 8 9 02 01 00 99 98

Contents

World of Difference

The timber wolf is a wonder dog. It is a dog with a difference. It is a wild dog — big and strong. It is the biggest wild dog in the world.

Male wolves grow larger than females. A male can grow so tall that his shoulders reach above a kitchen table. A very big wolf can weigh as much as a man.

All wolves have bristly fur and bushy tails, but they do not all look alike. They come in different sizes and colors. Some are black; some are white; others are tan or brown — even reddish. Most wolves,

In winter, a white wolf blends with the snow. In summer, you can spot it from far away.

5

The rare red wolf of the southeastern United States is smaller and lighter than most timber wolves.

however, are gray with streaks of other colors. For this reason, timber wolves are also called gray wolves.

Unlike many other animals, wolves establish close families. Parents and their young all live together in a pack of up to twenty or more. The pack travels together, feeds together, plays together, and sleeps together. An aunt or uncle of the pups sometimes joins the pack.

Wolf families are loving and loyal. The parents usually stay together their whole adult lives, helping each other care for their family and keep it safe.

As young wolves grow, they help their parents look after newborn pups. Some young wolves stay with their families three or four years. Then they might leave to find a mate and start a new pack — a family of their own.

WONDER WOLF

The wolf is an amazing animal! Here are some of its wonderful ways:

- A wolf can walk on slippery logs by spreading its toes.

- A wolf is a strong swimmer; it even chases beavers through the water.

- A wolf can sniff out clues to learn which wolves, male or female, have been near its home — and how long ago.

- A wolf will raise orphan pups as well as its own family.

7

Where in the World

You will not find wolves in town. Most wolves stay away from people. These wild dogs make wild places — the wilderness — their home.

Some packs are forest wolves that run among the shadows of the trees. Other packs are tundra wolves that race across treeless northlands.

Each wolf pack has a home territory that the wolves claim as their own. That territory is huge. An especially huge territory can be larger than a big city — even as big as 2,000 square miles

This wolf is looking over its territory. A wolf's home territory is huge — and wild.

With a big yawn, this wolf is ready to flop down on the snow for a nap. Another wolf in its family is already snoozing.

(5,000 square kilometers). When plenty of food is available, territories are smaller.

Most of the year, a wolf pack tours its territory. The wolves often travel up to 20 miles (32 km) a day. They hunt for food, take care of their families, and keep their territory free of other wolf packs.

Wolves do most of their business in the dim light of early morning and evening. When the sun is high, in the middle of the day, wolves usually lie down and sleep.

Many years ago, there were more wolves than there are now, and they lived in more places in the world. Today, wolves still live all across Canada and in several parts of Asia. There are few wolves, however, in Europe and in the United States — except in the state of Alaska.

HOW WOLVES EVOLVED

Native Americans believed that, when the northern lights danced, wolves came to visit. They saw the flashes of purple, red, and green light as signs of wolves bounding from sky to Earth.

Some scientists think wolves evolved from an ancient animal, called Mesocyon, that lived about thirty-five million years ago. The Mesocyon was a small "half-dog" with short legs and a long body. Like the wolf, it might have lived in packs.

World of the Hunter

Finding good food for the family keeps wolves very busy. Sometimes they nibble berries and bits of grass, but wolves need meat — so they are hunters.

Keen senses help wolves hunt. They can see as well as humans and can smell a deer more than a mile (km) away. They can hear noises from even farther away than that.

Wolves are built to chase the prey they sense. With their long, strong legs and big feet, they can run up to 40 miles (64 km) an hour and trot half a day without resting.

Long legs and big feet help a wolf run through the snow and brush.

13

This wolf is digging up an easy meal — food buried after an earlier hunt.

A lone wolf can catch animals smaller than itself, such as mice, squirrels, rabbits, and birds. With its pack, a wolf can go after animals much bigger than itself, such as deer, moose, buffalo, and musk-ox.

Wolves hunting in a pack often work as a team. They might take turns chasing their prey to tire it out, or half the pack might chase the prey toward the other half. Then they usually trap the prey by forming a circle around it.

After a successful hunt, the wolves feed. They often bury some of their prey to use for food on days when hunting is poor. They also carry some of the meat back to pups that are too young to join in the hunt. In the world of the hunter, the entire pack shares the prey.

DINNER ON THE RUN

A wolf spots a mouse. The wolf sneaks forward. Its eyes are fixed; its muscles are tense. Slowly, softly, carefully, it creeps. The wolf is ready to dash, but it hopes to move closer first.

The mouse spots the wolf. The mouse freezes. The wolf freezes, too. Suddenly, the mouse bolts, and the wolf leaps after it. In seconds, the mouse is gone — and the wolf has had another dinner on the run!

15

World of Words

Wolves talk. They whimper, bark, growl, and howl. They use their bodies to say things, too. Talking helps them live and hunt together.

Wolves howl for many reasons. The wind can carry the long, loud cries of a howling wolf more than 4 miles (6 km).

One pack might warn another to stay out of its territory by howling. Wolves in a pack also howl when they hunt. They howl to get ready for a hunt, to keep in touch during the hunt, and to celebrate after a successful hunt.

A pup asks for food by licking the nose and mouth of an older wolf.

Howling helps wolves in the forest find each other.

When a wolf leaves its pack, it howls "good-bye." Then it goes off and howls for a mate. If another wolf hears the howl, it answers. Sometimes, wolves even answer people — when they are howling like wolves.

Growls and snarls make good threats. Bared teeth and wrinkled noses make even better ones. When one wolf threatens another, it also raises its ears and tail and stares hard. Then, it fluffs out its fur, raises its back, and straightens its legs to look bigger and taller than it really is.

The wolf being threatened will usually flatten its ears, close its mouth, lower its body, and tuck its tail between its legs. It might even roll over, tummy up, and flop its head back to say "you win" — without making a sound.

PUT ON A HAPPY FACE

If you were a happy wolf, you would show it — and your whole pack would know it.

Your eyes would shine. Your ears would point forward. Your mouth would open, and your tongue would dangle out. You would leap and yip, and your whole body would jiggle with joy.

The happy sight would please your mother. Her tail would wag and her tongue would lick your nose to say "I love you" in wolf talk.

19

New World

These three-week-old pups are cozy in their den. They are different colors, but they all have the same mother.

Newborn wolf pups make spring special. Before they arrive, a mother wolf must find a place to have her pups. She looks for one that is shielded from wind and rain and is safe from danger. It might be a tunnel, a cave, a hollow log, or a cozy nook among some thick shrubs.

The mother wolf and her pack might make a new den, or they might look for a used one. In the frozen north, wolves have used the same caves for hundreds of years.

When it is time for the mother wolf to give birth, the whole pack gathers outside

Caring for new pups is a full-time job for a mother wolf.

the den. Throwing their heads back, the wolves howl a welcome to each pup. Then they lick one another and wag their tails to celebrate the births.

Up to eleven tiny pups might be born, each weighing only as much as a loaf of bread. The pups cannot hear or see their new world right away. Their mother stays close to keep them safe and warm and to feed them milk from her body.

For about three weeks, the mother wolf lives in the den with her pups. Her mate and other wolves in the pack bring food to her.

By the fourth week, the pups are able to spend some time outside the den. If anything scares them, they pop back in. Another wolf might "babysit" for a while so the pups' mother can rest.

DEEP IN THE DEN

Few people enter wolf dens, but one man did. He crawled through a hole the size of a bed pillow. Then he crept through a narrow underground tunnel.

After crawling 6 feet (2 meters), he came to a smooth hollow where an adult wolf had slept.

From that point, the tunnel turned sharply and sloped upward. The man followed it another 6 feet (2 m). There he found a second hollow that was once a cradle for wolf pups.

Small World

Hawks and eagles soar overhead. They are watching and waiting to snatch a wolf pup. The wolves, however, are watching and waiting, too, standing guard as their pups bob in and out of the den. Wolves keep their guard up even when the pups — at only two months old — leave the den for good.

As wolf pups sleep and eat with the other wolves, they become part of the pack. Pups and young wolves chase each other and play together. The younger ones follow the older ones around.

At two months old, a wolf pup is ready to start exploring its world. It might live for thirteen years or more.

The small world of wolf pups grows as they grow. The pack takes them farther and farther from the den, and older wolves start to teach them the ways of the wild.

Wolves are strict teachers. They growl if pups do not behave. If the pups are really bad, the older wolves bite them.

Besides learning to drink from lakes and streams, wolf pups learn to sniff around for signs of prey.

Many times a day, wolf parents knock over their pups and hold them down for a moment to teach them who the boss is.

By late fall, the pups are big enough, and smart enough, to start traveling. They learn how huge their territory really is when they follow the pack on hunting trips.

The pups walk, one by one, in line behind the adults. When snow falls, they step right into the footprints of the bigger wolves to make traveling in a bigger world a little easier.

WARNING: DANGER

A wolf pack was sleeping when, suddenly, its leader jumped up and growled. Its mate growled, too.

The mother wolf urged her pups to follow her as she raced to the den. The father wolf came last, nipping at a slow-moving pup. When all the pups were inside the den, their parents lay down at the opening.

Heavy footsteps pounded the ground above, but the den was quiet inside. The wolves stayed there until the people — the enemies they feared the most — were gone.

Fun World

One wolf pup leaps in front of another. Its front legs are down. Its rear end is up. Its tail is wagging furiously. It is saying, "Come on. Let's play!" Then the two pups run off together.

Like human children, wolf pups play a lot. They tumble and wrestle, pretending to fight. They often take turns chasing each other, too.

Pups play stick games. One pup grabs a twig and teases another wolf with it, which usually leads either to a chase or a game of tug-of-war.

These young wolves are running and playing — exercise to keep them healthy.

29

Ravens tease wolves for fun and for food. Sometimes they snatch meat away from them.

A wolf pup will often play alone. It might chew sticks or chase its tail. Racing and leaping, it snaps at bees and butterflies, or it pounces on flowers or on leaves that are tumbling in a breeze. Sometimes it just rolls over — and over and over.

30

As they grow, wolf pups race and chase for hours before they get tired. They play hard. Then, they take long, deep naps.

Playing is fun. It teaches pups to watch, listen, and react quickly. It exercises their muscles and helps the pups grow strong. It trains them to run fast and far and helps them learn how to hunt.

Playing together makes pups feel closer to each other — and to the adult wolves that play with them. Play helps the whole pack learn to live and work together.

RAVEN TAG

Where there are wolves, there are often ravens. These big, black birds like wolves. They like to grab leftovers from wolf hunts — and they like to play.

Ravens play with each other, sliding down snowbanks, passing sticks beak to beak, and turning somersaults in the air.

They also play by teasing wolves. Ravens dive at the wolves, then speed away. They peck at the wolves' tails. They even play "catch-me-if-you-can" by getting the wolves to chase them.

Glossary

bristly — having short, stiff hairs.

den — a cave or other place where a wild animal makes its home or hides from danger.

evolve — to change form gradually over a long period of time.

newborn — a baby animal that was just born or born a short time ago.

orphan — a young animal that has lost both its mother and father.

pack — (n) a group of animals of the same kind that live together.

shielded — covered or protected from danger in some way, as with a screen or shield.

snarl — to growl in a fierce way with the teeth showing.

territory — the area in which an animal or group of animals finds food and makes its home.

tundra — a large area of flat, treeless land in Arctic regions.

wilderness — a large area with few people, where plants and animals live in a wild, natural state.

Index